displaced.

Ari Para

BookLeaf Publishing

Presentation by *BookLeaf Publishing*

Web: www.bookleafpub.com

E-mail: info@bookleafpub.com

ISBN: 9789357213035

First edition 2023

I am from...

I am from a country of secrets. I am from a land still grieving. I am from a land bursting with culture.

I come from a strong mother. I come from a brave father. I find my strength and bravery through my sister. I come from an anxious family, resilient and motivated, yet perpetually broken.

In the place that I am from, I wake to the sound of hot oil burning on the stove. In the place that I am from, the kettle boils my favourite tea. In the place that I am from, I ride my bike to the market at 5AM to buy fresh milk to drink and cook with. In the place that I am from, we rise with the sun and rest when it sets. In the place that I am from, I dodge metal sheets covered with yoghurt soaked chillies while playing with the neighbour's dog.

I am from a village with a temple at its core, the sounds of bells ringing and vibrating through all the houses it inhabits. I am from a home that has seen more loss than was fair, but still dares to dream a more joyful future. In the place that I am from, everyone knows everyone, there is no room for secrets. In the place that I am from, incense burns almost all day long, the sweet smoke filling us with hope.

What we wanted

We all just wanted to grow up as children in the homeland, fragments of our parent's lives buried into our own, be raised in the village they so fondly call home. We all just wanted to know what it would have been like to grow up with people just like us, who had parents who thought like ours, who had the same rules to live by like us, who were just as limited, just as liberated, as us. We all just wanted the option to stay.

Boxers & High Heels

The first time I wrote this poem, I wrote it by hand in a journal I kept safe and private. It was my favourite poem. When I found out that other people had been going through my journals, reading my words without my permission, I ripped it up in two. I have been trying to find the same words ever since. I know I will never be able to replicate it perfectly, edited down to perfection, the way that I had it last time, but I can try to find the words. The process of trying to find the words has been painful. I think I am grieving that lost poem.

But...If there is anything that I have learned int the past couple of years, it is that I must keep trying to find the words, because these words hold power.

Boxers & High Heels.

When I first came out as trans, I started to clear out my closet. I wanted to get rid of every feminine thing in my room - my makeup, my earrings, my dresses, my skirts - all of it. Some of them were easy to get rid of. Others were harder. I didn't let myself feel the pain of losing my old self, or feel the pain of feeling like I had to lose my old self in order for people to take me seriously. I got rid of almost everything until I looked down at my closet and saw my favourite pair of red high heels. 5 inches high, strappy, patterned, elevated to perfection. I started to cry.

The next day, I wore my velvety purple lipstick, my paisley skirt with my tight white crop top, a cardigan hiding my shame. Shame I felt for dressing how I used to dress, how I liked to dress. Was I lying to myself?

I ran out of my home, didn't want my queer roommates to see me in drag. I got to work, a place I had just come out in, and dodged the stares from my colleagues. After a whole summer dressed in button downs, binders and boxers, here I was wearing a bra. A skirt. Makeup. They were just as confused as I was.

On my way back to the lunch room after my smoke break I heard the whispers.

"I honestly don't think she's trans."
"I feel like she's just saying it to be trendy."
"She's lying! Are you joking, did you see that skirt?"

"What boy wears makeup?"
"Should we be saying he or she? Or they?"
"What do you think, is she lying or just delusional?"

Lying or delusional.
It had to be one or the other. Questioning had no space to exist in their binary.

I circled the halls a few times before I could muster the courage to enter the break room, head held as high as my strappy high heels.

When I got home, I ran into the bathroom and washed my face, scrubbed it clean, scrubbed it dry until there was not an ounce of mac cosmetics left on my skin. I ran into my room, buried my head into a pillow and stayed there until work the next day.

I was high for the rest of that summer.

I didn't wear makeup again for another 3 years.

Addicted to a memory

Addicted to a memory, all eyes on me,
All these things that I've done, always in my
head.
Always leaving,
Always love.

Anybody there? Anyone, anyone?
Are you listening? Army of one.

Brown girls, brown skinned girls, bruised and
scarred, bulletproof.

Burn, burn, burn your life down.
Bury a friend, buzzkill.

Call if you need me or call it off.
Came here for love but you can't have
everything.
Careful.
Careful.
Centre of Attention.
Champagne's for celebrating, chasing cheap
thrills...
Cheers chellama, cherie amour.

Daydreaming til the day I die.
The day you died because you wanted to…
Dead and gone.
Dead on arrival.
Dead wrong.
Dearly departed, don't be so hard on yourself.

Empty apartment, empty cups, empty space.
Enakenna yaarum illaye, en iniya thanimaye

Everybody hates me, everything's an illusion.
Everything's magic.
Everything will be alright.

Photographs

Photographs are the only way to get them to open up. We sit and we create space for them to share but they still want to shield us from the dangers they experienced. They are still trying to protect us, forgetting that we still live in a world that will never be safe for us, only a bit safer than the last place. They don't realize that their history is ours too, that their trauma flows in our veins, that we need to heal what was done to them just as much as they do.

Perhaps they have lost access to those memories, perhaps the photos are all that is left of their youthful innocence, the days before the war, now rifts in their minds and hearts. The possibilities they once had stolen from them, something completely out of their control. My father talks about leaving home for the first time forever at 19, something I ignored the weight of when I was leaving home at 19. Being home reminds me of the pains and struggles of their everyday lives, different from mine but manifested the same. I hope to one day lessen the burdens on their backs, take the weight of the pain in their hearts and make it my own, just to give them a break.

Family Photos

We are in Pittsburgh. I am five years old, you are three. We have just met a family member that already feels like home. This is how young children get along. I am at the top of the playground, ready to shout, "I'M KING OF THE WORLD" just as my mother takes out her disposable camera and hits the button that snaps that moment in time, forever.

My sister and I look at the picture decades later and laugh at my attention seeking tendencies, at the size of her cheeks, at the poor family members standing nearby, confused, having to endure our chaotic energy. We think about all the similar photos we have to this one…remember our first trip to the CN tower? Or that photo of me lying on the floor, hand to a bottle of milk like it was whiskey? Remember that photo of you on the bed, rolls on rolls on rolls?

I remember a quote I read recently, something about how we are only ever dead when the last person who has a memory of us dies. How long do you think we'll last in the memories of others? Do you think it could be decades? Or are we doomed to end sooner than we had hoped?

Fuck Me Up

Faint of heart, fake happy, fake love.
Fool for you, but then again I fall for anything.
For a pessimist, I am pretty forgiving.

Fast in my car, February air, feeling sorry,
feeling it still.
For the first time I am finding it hard to smile.
If I find you again, I'll fix you, fix you up.

The fragrant taste of rain, full moon, fully alive.
The funeral of the future.
How flawless.

I still remember the flower, the flower in your
hair.
Fly away during my finest hour…fuck me up.

Get back in my life right when I'm getting over
you.
Girls like you want to give me hell.
Glad you exist, glowing, godly woman.

Goodbye, goodbye, goodbye, my friend. Go off,
go on girl.

Gospel salt stuck in my teeth at the grateful
graveyard, the greatest grip.
Call it growing pains.
Call it a guardian angel.
Call it a guiding light.

It ends with me howling for you.
That's how the world works.
That's how to be human.
That's how to be sick.
That's how you save a life.

I guess I just feel like… I hate everybody.
(ILYSB)
I'm afraid of men, and I'm a mess and I miss
you.
I'm so tired… is there more? Does there have to
be?
I swear this time I mean it, I wanna be yours.
At least just for a moment.
Just say you're not into it.
Just stay here tonight.

Second Chances

Am I ready for another chance in the ring?
Have I healed enough from the competition of
my past?
Am I over the pain of broken promises and
hopes halted shut?
I am.
I am.
I am.

This much I know…

This time around, I won't fight for those who are determined to see me fail to lighten their own misery.

This time around, I won't wait around for those who say they aren't like the others to prove themselves wrong.

This time around, I will stand unwavering in my truth, only changing when I grow, only moving when I must.

This time around I will heal on my own time, slowly forgetting that there was ever a time that I didn’t listen to my own intuition.

Life's deep end

Curiously yearning for a better tomorrow.
Nostalgic nuisance breeding beautiful memories.
Treading into life’s uncertain deep end.
Left constantly questioning life’s curve balls.

9AM Shift

I practically jump out of bed for the 9AM shift at the pool. It's summer, my 18th birthday weeks away…this is the summer of freedom.

I rush downstairs, grabbing the keys off the wall hook before I even touch the ground, "I'm leaving for work!" I call back to Amma and Appa.

"Hold on…we'll drop you off."

I stop. I turn. "Why?" Appa looks at the ground as he answers, "We need it, we're going somewhere."

The sun is beating down, illuminating the kitchen, forcing happiness and acceptance on me before I have a chance to feel it myself. It is hot, too hot, and for someone who loves the heat, it takes a lot to feel too hot. Uncomfortably hot, especially wearing just a swimsuit and my lifeguard jersey on top.

The smell of chicken curry in the kitchen behind him softens the blow - my favourite food. Here I was, declaring I was leaving instead of asking for permission. Who did I think I was? Will they always see me this way? Will they always see me as a woman, needing to ask for permission in order to do anything, no matter my age? "As it should be", they would say.

Why does everyone around me think they can dictate my life? I know that as long as I am under their roof this is how it will be, but what about the others? What invisible rules do they consider when they look at me? Look at my body, at the colour of my skin?

The birds are singing, but the melody is interrupted by the sound of lawnmowers revving up, signalling the beginning of yet another dreadful day in suburbia. I see my white neighbours outside their homes talking to each other, a friendship my parents could never access, nor would they want to.

The kitchen table blocks me as I ask once again if I can take the car, my car, to work like I always do. They tell me they need it, but I know they're lying. They've been checking the mileage, they know I've been leaving work during my lunch break, gone to see "god knows how"...so they take my freedom away.

The back door is to my right, slid open to reveal a net caught with bugs who can't escape - relatable. The front door is to my left…I should just leave. I'm late for work. I forget the portrait of Shiva behind me, the TV blaring Kollywood songs, forget the existence of the fireplace on this hot hot day. The cold tile floor cools me down, reminds me nothing will come of this rage. The chandelier above me hangs in the balance like my freedom, trapped in a house where I will never be enough.

Killing my Time

Killing me, killing my time.
I know I'm the last thing on your mind.

Leave me.
Leave my body.
Leave the door open.

Let me love you or let me down slowly. Fuck it, let's call it off.
A little bit more time's enough, little talks, just a little too much.

Maybe I'm afraid. Maybe I need you.
Meet me at our spot, meet me in the sky.
I am miles apart from the mind eraser, that miracle mirror that leaves me miserable at best.
These misguided ghosts fill me up with loneliness.
These ghosts make me feel naked, nasty, natural, needy.

Make me feel like I'm never going to give you up.
I'll never leave this bed with you by my side.
Just promise me you'll never let me go.

Never mind. Let's break up.

Nights with you feel like no air, no angel,
nobody's home, no light, no light, no light…

(After all, only the lonely survive.)

Fever Dream

It is 5AM in Jaffna. I wake up thinking how we could be their bridge, reversing intergenerational curses to allow them to be freer, lighter and better. We could be their bridge, helping them see what was too hard for their parents to see, easing them through the transition of being bred from well meaning parents who just didn't have enough time to learn the rules of this country before bringing them into it.

A heavy thought for the morning. I stretch, take a deep breath, look up at the sky and then down at my feet, seeing the beautifully coloured flowers blooming. I am reminded of the last time I received flowers.

As I received those flowers from the hands of the woman I knew was giving me a bad rep in the theatre program at my university, smiling at me, saying I did a wonderful job when I saw her laughing at me in the front row, trying to make me corpse, I am reminded of the fact that actors first started to bow on stage so that the compliments and applause would go over their heads, making sure their ego's didn't inflate. I immediately think of my actions earlier that night while she presents me with her fake smile, flowers and comments, trying to remember how far I bowed. I realized then with a panic that I didn't bow that far, mostly because working on this show was exhausting, it wasn't something I was proud of. I wonder if she saw my half bow and prescribed it all to a huge ego, not the recognition that I was raised to move small, that in my family, moving slow and being small is a sign of respect, of knowing one's place, something that surely went over her head. Even now, I can't bring myself to laugh at the irony, the memory is too painful.

My thoughts are interrupted by a cup full of rice.

"Here, try this," my aunt shoves a cup in front of me.

"What is it?"

"Just try it!"

I take the cup from Asai Mami's hands and peer inside. I see a cool broth filled with rice. I take a sip - it's delicious.

"What is this?"

My dad is quick to jump in, “Don’t tell her!” He warns his older sister, knowing that he would be the one to face my hangry wrath later.

“It’s kanji. It’s all the leftover foods from yesterday mixed together with water.”

“I told you not to tell her!”

“Why should she not tell me? Why don’t you want me to know?”

“We thought you were too Canadian for village scraps.”

I find it funny that they think I am too “modern” for village living. As if their blood doesn’t run through these veins. As if my melanin wasn’t made for this tropical heat, as if there was any other place in the world that I would rather be than right here, surrounded by coconut trees and jack fruit and garbage fires and stray dogs visiting house to house for a chance at the scraps my family thought I was too good to eat.

Jaded Kill

A blind convulsion, determined exclusion,
finding gain, hate internalized, jaded kill.
Loathing melanin, neglecting our pain.
Quiet remembering, silent tears.
Understanding violence without xenogogue.
Yesterday's zeitgeist.

Part Time Woman

Pray for me.
The problem with me is that the big picture is
always too hard for me to see.
I'll just sit here and quarantine and chill until I
find out what I've been missing.
Remind me to forget, reckless lover, the reason
that I need rescuing.
Rewind the tape on this tragic life, let me rewrite
the stars.
Sacrifices they say. I'll be sad forever, definitely
sad tonight.
Safe inside they say.
Sariya, idhu thavara?

Let me fall into this slow fade, slow grenade,
slow hands crushing me to death, slow it down,
slow my life down, slow me down. Take my
breath away.

304

A few days after my grandmother died, my grandfather was heard singing to her empty bed in their room, asking her spirit…"What am I going to do without you?"

That night, we decided to play his favourite card game. We have been playing the same game everyday for the past 296 days. We all get together, with our afternoon tea and biscuits, remnants of their colonial past everpresent, playing Monopoly Deal, Settlers of Catan, 304, for hours and hours until the loneliness has no space left to exist in his heart.

My Ancestors Would Laugh

My ancestors would laugh at the worries crowding my mind. They would shiver with excitement and giggles at the thoughts that keep me up at night.

"Child, you don't even know what's coming", mocking me the way I mock reality TV. "Life is just not that serious!! Embrace!"

I bet my ancestors have all made up by now, throwing away the pains and fights of yesterday bred through intergenerational trauma, now united in their confidence in my future, because they know that I can't be.

Wow, this lineage of strong women that I come from.

Is this mourning? Is this grieving?

The way she looked at me. The way she knew it was time to go. How okay with it she was. How hard she gripped my hand when she could no longer speak. How scared she must have been.

My ancestors are finally reunited, the best of friends, anger forgotten, souls forgiven. My ancestors would laugh at my pain, knowing that in a few minutes, months, or years, it'll cease to matter. My ancestors are waiting for me. My ancestors are on the other side of that door, ready to welcome me with open arms. There is nothing to fear. What would I do without my ancestors? Without their wisdom. Without their experience. That strong lineage of strong women. It is in our blood to embrace pain with strength. It is our birthright. It is my birthright.

Unknown to U

Unknown to U is U love U.
U leave me unsatisfied, feeling ugly when U prioritize U.
U make me feel lonely. U make me feel like nobody.
U are the reason we are through, U have no one to blame but U.

Thevasam / Oore party

The sound of teenagers laughing in the
basement, hopped up on candy and pop.
Drunk uncles outside, fighting the urge to dance
their trauma away.
Gossiping aunties judging each other's children
and spouses.
These are the sounds that fill the oore party,
really a thevasam, but transformed over the
years to include as much fun as possible.

Most of the men drink in secret and make fools of themselves in public. The women will watch and shake their heads. The kitchen will be filled with people cooking, laughing, smiling, trying to forget the real reason we get together every year.

Not just a grandfather, but an aunt and her children too. How an unexpected death turned into an attempted murder suicide. Carrying her sleeping twins into the trunk of her car, fainting in the front seat, garage door sealed with the engine on. The fact that we visited them the day before they died. That we could tell something was wrong but didn't think it would be the last day we would ever see them again. That this was a norm that we were supposed to accept at twelve years old.

It's been years now since it happened, and though she survived before starving herself in a hospital, then in prison, we all still get together every year, spending as little time praying for their souls as possible before we start jumping on the trampoline, swimming in the pool, running and claiming a spot on the couch in the basement before the other 30 cousins crash down into us. And we laugh and laugh and try our best to forget the real reason we are all there.

Walking with a ghost

Wake me up from this nightmare.
You do, but I still wake up alone.
I wake up exhausted.
I wake up wondering
WHERE THE HELL ARE MY FRIENDS?

Sometimes I still wish you were here.
Even though together we walked through hell,
I am left walking with your ghost.
Walk me home, walk with me til I'm dead.

No more wasted time, no longer wasting a
moment wishing you were gay.
We are broken, but we belong together.

Yes, I'm changing.
But one thing never will.
You are the one.
You've got my love.

Nothing Softens These Wounds

Nothing softens the wounds of my grandmothers like the resilience of my existence. The bravery I contain to take on more then I am ready to, because I know I am capable. How I see myself in both of them, and they me. The way we shake up the world's views of us. The way we force others to pay attention to us. The way we run the men in our lives, because we refuse to give in to their weakness. We are stronger together, even with most of us gone and the rest of us leaving. We are connected by that invisible spool, inked into my right thigh, reminding me that the threads of fate will keep me courageous and brave.

Nothing softens the wounds of my grandmothers like the resilience of my existence. My sweetness disguised as abrasive, as messy, as emotional, as angry, as volatile, inconsistent. My sweetness presents itself in intensity, in a roughness that I don't have the language to describe. My ancestors learn from me as I learn from them. The sweetness of my existence is proof of theirs.

The traits I’ve inherited from my grandparents help soften the blows of this existence. My paternal grandfather’s lucky horseshoe shaped forehead that I’ve inherited paired with his depression reminds me to stay humble. My paternal grandmother’s physical and emotional pain that I’ve inherited reminds me to stay brave. My maternal grandmother’s strength and abrasiveness that I've inherited remind me to stay true to me. My maternal grandfather’s competitiveness that I’ve inherited reminds me that nothing is permanent, an important lesson from my last living grandparent. Alone, fierce, and resilient. The wisdom I have acquired from these humans… how lucky I am.

I couldn’t have asked for better guides to navigate this life.

Liberated Spirit

Nostalgic nuisance breeds beautiful memories.
Chaotic leaves spiralling, bewildering beauty.
Bountiful sunshine beaming vibrant love.
False spring bringing immense hope.
Broken agreements ignite fractured
relationships.

How much longer will
the land hold me up without
anything returned?

Leaves changing to red.
Winter, taking it away.
Spring's bright renewal.

How much longer will
the world maintain it's beauty
before we end it?

Silent prayers feeding angry souls.
Cautious temptations filling tired bodies.
Crowded hearts emptying purposeless notions.
Ugly thoughts leaving tired minds.
Liberated spirit - find loving days.

www.ingramcontent.com/pod-product-compliance
Lightning Source LLC
Chambersburg PA
CBHW051749130826
49812CB00033B/1069
* 9 7 8 9 3 5 7 2 1 3 0 3 5 *